**NO,
YOU'RE NOT
GOING CRAZY!**

# NO, YOU'RE NOT GOING CRAZY!

**VIVIAN I. POTTER**

XULON PRESS

Xulon Press
2301 Lucien Way #415
Maitland, FL 32751
407.339.4217
www.xulonpress.com

© 2019 by Vivian I. Potter

All rights reserved solely by the author. The author guarantees all contents are original and do not infringe upon the legal rights of any other person or work. No part of this book may be reproduced in any form without the permission of the author. The views expressed in this book are not necessarily those of the publisher.

Unless otherwise indicated, Scripture quotations taken World Messianic Bible (WMB)–*public domain.*

Printed in the United States of America.

ISBN-13: 978-1-5456-6591-6

My immeasurable gratitude goes first to my Heavenly Father, my King Yeshua, and the Holy Spirit, who placed this on my heart to complete.

To my Little Monkey and my Little Wiggly Worm, you are truly gifts from God. I am so proud of the strong young women you've become and I feel privileged to have been chosen as your mother. I love you, my babies.

To my promised one, I have loved you from before I was born. You are so worth the wait!!

To all those who have been for and against me, I give you my deepest thanks as well.

# Table of Contents

FOREWORD . . . . . . . . . . . . . . . . . . . . . . . . . . . . . ix

**PART I**
Chapter 1: My Story. . . . . . . . . . . . . . . . . . . . . . . . . . 1
Chapter 2: Hurricane Andrew – Goodbye Florida, Hello Caribbean. . . . . . . . . . . . . . . . . . . . 5
Chapter 3: Back to the USA. . . . . . . . . . . . . . . . . . . 9
Chapter 4: Hello Florida – Again . . . . . . . . . . . . . . 11
Chapter 5: The Turning Point . . . . . . . . . . . . . . . . 13

**PART II**
Chapter 6: What is Narcissism? . . . . . . . . . . . . . . 17
Chapter 7: Gaslighting – No, You're Not Going Crazy!. . . . . . . . . . . . . . . . . . . . . . 35
Chapter 8: Emotional Intelligence – Who Has It?

**PART II**
Chapter 9: Your Healing. . . . . . . . . . . . . . . . . . . . . 47
Chapter 10: Final Words…. . . . . . . . . . . . . . . . . . . . 51

REFERENCES. . . . . . . . . . . . . . . . . . . . . . . . . . . . . 53

# Foreword

I would like to first state that although both men and women fall prey to narcissists, this book is primarily addressed to women (but men can glean some gems from this as well).

I would also like to state that this book was made with no intention whatsoever of any male-bashing, most of all my ex-husband. If it comes across this way, I want to extend my sincerest apologies right now. I simply want to tell my story so that others in similar situations can relate and have hope of healing and empowerment. To that end, all references to people and locations have been changed to protect the innocent and the guilty.

# PART I

## CHAPTER 1:

# My Story

It has been said that little girls grow up to marry someone like their fathers. Although I can't say for certain that my father was a narcissist, since he was a private person, my mother never revealed as much, and they are both long deceased so I can't ask either, I can say he shared some similarities with my ex-husband, i.e. love for baseball, financial security, and silent treatments.

I met my ex-husband after just turning 22 and having just moved from New York to the Rocky Mountain area. Both he and a relative of mine were actively serving in the military on the same installation. My relative invited him to his home for the holidays and that's where we met. I was the last to arrive, since it was snowing that day and I was not used to driving in the snow. When I walked in, I saw him sitting at the far corner of the sofa with his hands folded in his lap. I thought to myself, "He looks like a little boy!" If I had only known...

Fast forward a couple of months...we are now dating. Fast forward a couple more months...I find out he's engaged to be married to someone from his hometown. Needless to say, I was devastated. He insisted he felt "obligated" to marry her since they had been dating a couple of years and "it was expected," although he said he didn't want to. I remember one night at his apartment the phone rang. He said he knew it was her and told me to watch how he was going to make her break up with him. He manipulated the conversation so that, indeed, she did break up with him. I was astonished he would play this game with her and not just tell her how he felt, but I stayed quiet. You see, I had already fallen in love with him - or so I thought. First red flag.

A few months later we're living together and although we're in the honeymoon phase, I start to notice some patterns begin to develop: silent treatments followed by yelling, sleeping at the foot of the bed, hanging out with the "guys" and coming home drunk, all after having a seemingly beautiful day together. More red flags. Are those sirens I hear?

Two years later he gets orders to Florida. I had always wanted to go there, so this should be great news, right? Maybe it would've been if I didn't find out from my mother and had it confirmed by other family members. I was the last he informed, with no invitation

*My Story*

to accompany him. Now I'm hearing, "Danger! Danger!" along with the sirens and red flags.

I was finishing up my undergraduate degree when it was time for him to leave. I invited myself to move to Florida, which I left 2 months later (call it starry-eyed or stupidity - I'll let the reader use discernment). Since he was living in the dorms, he had to "scramble" to get an apartment off-base. This wasn't so easy because he was single and not a senior NCO (Non Commissioned Officer). Now you'd think would come the proposal, right? Wrong! He flew his father out to list him as a dependent so he can move out of the dorm. Those sirens keep getting louder and now I'm seeing flashing lights.

A big blow came when I found out I was pregnant with our daughter. When I told him, he was completely silent. I remember going to one of his friend's house shortly after the news and I was sitting on the couch talking with his friend's wife while he and his friend were standing in front of us, facing us. I knew he had just told his friend because they both were silent, staring at me. Did I sense resentment oozing from their pores? Oh, the sirens are so loud!!

Several months later we buy our first house (correction, HE buys the house - still no talk of marriage). My mom flew in the very day I go into labor - which lasted over 30 hours. Now, I understand many men don't know what to do to comfort their partners at this difficult time, but all he did was sit in a corner. He didn't say anything to me, didn't hold my hand, didn't even show any emotion. I got more comfort from the seemingly thousands of personnel who came to check me - and, of course, my mom.

Time for delivery! The doctor decided on a C-section and he was allowed in the operating room with me. When our daughter was born, he showed no emotion - towards me or our daughter. The doctor was more excited!

We came home from the hospital on a Friday and he received a call from his friend. I had answered the phone in the kitchen and since he was in the bedroom, I told him to pick up the extension there. Since the TV was on, I couldn't hear if he had picked up the phone. So after a few minutes, I pick up the receiver from the counter to make sure and I hear his friend tell him, "Come on! Just say you're coming to my house. I'll lend you a shirt so we can go out." I was furious! He was going to hang out on the very night his daughter came home, knowing I'd need help getting out of bed after my operation?? He didn't go out when I confronted him about this - that night. He did go out the following night. Where are the aspirin? My headache is so fierce from all the sirens!! Little did I know the best was yet to come.

## CHAPTER 2:

# Hurricane Andrew – Goodbye Florida, Hello Caribbean

August 24, 1992 is a day I'll never forget - my first hurricane. Andrew came in at a Category 5 with 165 mph winds, the eye going right over our city. Needless to say, the whole city was devastated and the base practically leveled. The whole county experienced a mandatory evacuation and I and my then 9-month daughter drove north to stay with a friend of a friend outside of Orlando. He, in turn, stayed with friends about 20 minutes away because he said he needed to stay close in the event of a military recall.

I remember driving back once we were allowed back into the county and seeing the devastation as soon as I crossed the county line. It looked like a war zone! I was drinking my tears by the time I got to our home, which for the most part was still standing, although there were gaping holes from several areas of the roof and the wall separating two bedrooms was knocked down, now making them one room. I was completely baffled at how so much damage can be done in such a short amount of time.

Since we were homeless, I needed to think of our daughter, so I went to stay with my mother for several months until things were sorted. He did provide for us financially during that time by forwarding us advances from the homeowners insurance. One thing I must give to him and would never take away from him is that he has always been financially responsible with his family, both his own and his parents. He is a good financial provider.

Now that the base was virtually destroyed, all personnel were being given the assignments of their choice – unheard of for the military. He chose a location stateside until he heard from a friend who worked a special duty assignment in the Caribbean. He was told there was an opening for a 3 year assignment where he was. He's all excited because this is the only way he'd be able to get closer to his family. I'm not completely sold on it because now he's saying I'd love the area, meanwhile just a few short years ago he told me I would hate it and never adjust. Hmmm...just what was I getting myself into??

Well, long story short, the 3 year assignment turned into a 6.5 year sentence, since he got another special duty assignment. During this time we did get married. He never came out and asked me; he mentioned in a letter to me while he was on a temporary assignment that he had thought about it. Stupid and desperate me, I ran with that and started making plans for our wedding. Since we now had our house built, I just wanted a small ceremony with family and friends at home. He wanted to have it done at the courthouse. Was he ashamed of me? He agreed to my suggestion of a destination wedding, but didn't tell his family about it. The only one who congratulated me upon our return was his niece, who didn't know until I told her. At a happy time as this, I really felt neglected, especially since he continued hanging out on the weekends, and unappreciated as a wife and homemaker. This is when I truly felt like a single mother. This is when my depression started. This is also when I started my emotional eating, which has now led to a diagnosis of intestinal impermeability (aka leaky gut), e-coli, and labrynthitis (a form of vertigo). I felt ugly and unloved. But stupid me thought the cause of our domestic problems was the place we lived, and if we were out of that place, things would improve. Boy was I wrong!!

## CHAPTER 3:

# Back to the USA

As his special duty assignment was coming to an end, he got orders to return stateside. Oddly enough, the orders were changed within a week to the northern east coast. I truly believe things happen for a reason and this is where I met my life-long best friend. Unfortunately during this wonderful time bonding with my new friend, my marriage continued to unravel. I still felt neglected and unappreciated. I also felt unrealistic expectations were unspokenly "understood." Not only did I work full-time and come home to cook, clean, and care for our growing family, but I finally went back to school to pursue a graduate degree. I had also encouraged him to finish his undergraduate degree and had devised a study schedule for us. It seemed to be going well, but I quickly noticed that he started to feel overwhelmed with his light course load and I felt obligated to help him with a class or two. But this stressful schedule did not stop him from leaving me alone on Friday and occasionally Saturday nights to hang out with "the guys." I truly felt so alone and my voice was not heard - not even in letters I would write him to express my feelings so as to avoid the yelling that more times than not came after our discussions. I felt I was expected to accept this way of life as normal; what was really happening was that I was slowly dying inside. I was losing myself and got crazy looks (and more yelling) if I tried to vocalize my feelings. I became so numb I didn't even hear the sirens anymore.

We finally finished our respective degree programs and I immediately set out to find employment using this degree. I did not want to stay up north (too cold) and expressed my desire to return to Florida, especially since his retirement from the military was coming up within a year. He said that was fine and I landed a position at a university in South Florida as an academic advisor. Within a few months our daughters and I moved to Florida while he stayed up north for 8 months to finish his military career. I was so torn at that time. I really wanted our family to be together, but not with the same treatment. So while I felt a sense of peace of not being around the neglect and yelling, I longed for us to be together. I thought that maybe this transition to civilian life would spark a change in him. Me - still the dreamer!!

## CHAPTER 4:

# Hello Florida – Again

Once he arrived after his retirement from the military, things definitely took a nosedive. He became increasingly moody, testy, and even more quick with his temper. Once he found a job he liked, he immediately made friends with like-minded people and started hanging out again. I was feeling more and more desperate and sought solace in my faith in God. His actions of defiance became progressively more bold as he saw I had a support system, like his seeking "friendship" with other women. Maybe he felt he was losing control over me? I definitely felt I was building a relationship with God and started relying on Him more and more.

I would ask God things like, "Why would anyone who loves someone treat them as if they were hated?", "How can I show him how much I love him?", "Have I done anything wrong?" I would surprise him with things I knew he liked, i.e. baseball tickets, etc., but he would either refuse to go or he would go reluctantly.

*No, You're Not Going Crazy!*

I felt he did not want to be with me and it seemed to me he lived his life as if he were single. Whenever I tried talking to him about this, I was either brushed off, yelled at, or ignored. I truly didn't know what to do... until the day arrived when things started to change.

**CHAPTER 5:**

# The Turning Point

I'll never forget that day...I was washing dishes and looking out the kitchen window. I said to God, "If you think I'm ready, show me who's really in my house." That is when I finally started seeing things for how they really were. He gradually brought back memories to my mind of occasions when things didn't go well and I, as usual, made excuses for it. But this time when I remembered them, it's as if God showed me the event from a different perspective, and it wasn't pretty. It was downright cruel, actually. It's as if God showed me who he is through His eyes. This is what helped me to start detaching myself emotionally from him and start healing. I was becoming repulsed. But at the same time, I drew closer to God for strength and wisdom as to what to do with this information.

I think I can safely speak for the majority of women when I say that when she has reached a certain breaking point in a relationship, she says, "That's enough. I'm done!" This is what happened to me several years later and we eventually divorced. The moment the judge said that this marriage is now dissolved, I felt an incredible weight lifted off me. This is where I really started getting myself back.

I did go through the gambit of emotions: denial, resentment, anger, and acceptance. Funny, I only grieved for about 5 minutes when we left the courtroom after the divorce. I didn't grieve for him, but for the marriage. It was, after all, the death of a marriage and that is sad. That is something I didn't want. But I came to realize I deserved to be in a reciprocal relationship where both parties are respected, heard, and appreciated.

I will say that as difficult as it was to relive and write these experiences here, I do not hate this person. Quite the contrary, I wish him happiness and I had calmly and respectfully told him as much. This admission, I feel, shocked him. Maybe he was expecting a fight or tears. But he was showing a pattern very typical of narcissists, which I will now explain.

# PART II

## CHAPTER 6:

# What is Narcissism?

Narcissism, in a nutshell, is where a person has an inflated sense of self-importance and will pursue gratification from vanity or egotistic admiration of his or her own attributes. Narcissism, believe it or not, has actually been classified as a personality disorder by the American Psychiatric Association ever since 1968 (Narcissistic Personality Disorder, 301.81, DSM-V: Diagnostic & Statistical Manual of Mental Disorders, 5th Edition, 2013). Although NPD is more prevalent in males (18 percent) than in females (6 percent), this mental illness is considered to be one of the least identified personality disorders.

It seems a bit harsh to state that narcissism could actually be a mental disorder, wouldn't you say? Actually, it isn't. It is actually considered one of the four Cluster B personality disorders, which is classified by dramatic, overly emotional or unpredictable thinking or behavior that affect a person's emotions and interpersonal relations. Other Cluster B personality disorders include antisocial personality disorder, borderline personality disorder, and histrionic personality disorder.

Lana Burgess in her article, "What are Cluster B Personality Disorders?", explains that according to the DSM-V, a personality disorder is an enduring pattern of inner experience and behavior that deviates from the norm of the individual's culture. This includes: being seen in 2 or more areas, such as cognition, affect, interpersonal functioning, and impulse control; inflexible and pervasive across a broad range of personal and social situations remaining consistent over time; severe enough to significantly impair the person's capabilities to develop meaningful relationships and psychological abilities to function in social, work or other areas of functioning; and stable and of long duration, with its onset being traced back to early adulthood or adolescence.

Some of the symptoms we will discuss may make you wonder if you yourself have this illness, but not to worry. While some symptoms may be common to many people at any given moment, a medical diagnosis is determined by seeing a consistent pattern of a combination of many behaviors over an extensive period of time. Personality disorders are diagnosed by a trained mental health professional (psychologist or psychiatrist) involving long-term psychotherapy. This is done by comparing symptoms and life history with those listed in the DSM-V and determining if they meet the criteria for a personality disorder diagnosis. As you can probably gather, prognosis for NPD patients is slow and there is a high dropout rate, since the vast majority of narcissistic people do not even feel they have a problem.

Interestingly, the exact cause of NPD is not known by researchers. While it is agreed that more research is needed on this subject, most subscribe to a biopsychosocial model of causation or promotion. Allow me to explain each in some detail.

In regards to biological and genetic factors, research has identified a structural abnormality in the brain of those with NPD, specifically less volume of gray matter in the left anterior insula and in the prefrontal cortex. These areas of the brain are associated with empathy, compassion, emotional regulation and cognitive functioning. The evidence suggests a compromised capacity for emotional empathy and regulation. Because of it's genetic nature, research suggests there is a slightly increased risk for this disorder to be hereditary.

Psychological factors involve how a person's personality and temperament are shaped by his or her environment and learned coping skills to deal with stress. In people with NPD, however, they exhibit excessive admiration that is never balanced with realistic feedback. In their formative years, evidence shows severe emotional abuse and have most likely learned manipulative behaviors from their parents or peers. Social factors include how a person interacts with family, friends and, especially in early development, other children. Many who have been diagnosed with NPD have had an impaired attachment to their primary caregivers in childhood. NPD can result in the child's perception of him or herself as unimportant and unconnected to others and can come to believe they have some personality defect that makes them unvalued and unwanted. These perceptions are often a result of childhood physical and/or sexual abuse and neglect.

**Narcissistic Abuse**

Narcissistic abuse is a form of emotional and psychological abuse, primarily inflicted by individuals who have either NPD or ASPD (Antisocial Personality Disorder), which are associated with lack of empathy or a conscience, respectively.

The statistics are truly staggering for those who have been diagnosed with either of these two disorders and those they affect. Current statistics show that approximately 3.3% of the population have ASPD and 6% have NPD. In the US alone, which has a population of approximately 326 million people, this would mean 10,758,000 people have ASPD and 19,560,000 have NPD. If each person narcissistically abuse just 5 people during their lives, this would amount to 53.8 and 97.8 people, respectively - a total of 151.6 million people in the United States alone emotionally abused by narcissism!

If we were to take this worldwide, we would see that out of the approximately 7.5 billion people in the world, 247.5 million show no conscience and 450 million show no empathy. Combine these figures and multiply that by the 5 affected people, we come up with an astonishing 3.4 BILLION PEOPLE - almost half of the world's population! Ladies, these are just the figures of those who have been diagnosed with these personality disorders. There are countless others walking among us who definitely show signs. These figures also do not include any children affected by these abusive relationships. If this doesn't indicate there is a serious, legitimate problem, then I don't know what does. It is extremely unfortunate that narcissistic abuse goes unnoticed by many because many times there are no visible signs. Because there may be no physical scars, many people do not even realize that what they're experiencing is a legitimate form of abuse until the damage has been done. But this does not make it any less real, any less painful, any less debilitating.

Narcissistic abuse is covert, and often disguised as love and care, but is anything but. It's not a single act of cruelty like an insulting comment, or verbal abuse interwoven with a string of profanities. It's the underhanded, gradual, and intentional erosion of a person's sense of self-worth. It is a combination of emotional and psychological abuse targeted at undermining a person's identity for the sole purpose of obtaining control for personal gain. Narcissistic abuse can involve patterns of dominance, manipulation, intimidation, emotional coercion, withholding, dishonesty, extreme selfishness, guilt mongering, rejection, stonewalling, gaslighting, financial abuse, extreme jealousy, and possessiveness. More details on these in a bit.

We must not ignore that a partner who never calls you a derogatory name and tells you he loves you every single day can be a narcissistic abuser. But all the love and concern for you won't lessen the damaging emotional and mental toll of the silent treatments when you assert your opinion or disagree. There are disapproving looks or criticisms over the most trivial things. There is the subtle, but constant treatment that has you feeling you are not good enough, and wholly incapable of pleasing your abuser for any length of time. The moments of kindness or the surprise bouquet of flowers do not erase the dizzying, circular conversations that exhaust and drain you into submission. When narcissistically abused, you can never express a differing opinion or suggest your partner isn't perfect or right.

The sweet gestures don't cancel out the hundreds of ways your compassion and love are exploited and used to manipulate you. These gestures actually make the unpredictable changing climate that shifts from kindness and tenderness to coldness and subtle cruelty, at times at lightning speed, more confusing and stressful.

In his book Why Does He Do That?, author Lundy Bancroft shows an example of how abuse can cause great psychological harm without the use of anger, yelling, or name calling: "...He can assault his partner psychologically without even raising his voice. He tends to stay calm in arguments, using his own evenness as a weapon to push her over the edge. He often has a superior or contemptuous grin on his face, smug and self-assured. He uses a repertoire of aggressive conversational tactics at low volume, including sarcasm, derision - such as openly laughing at her - mimicking her voice, and cruel cutting remarks. Like Mr. Right, he tends to take things she has said and twist them beyond recognition to make her appear absurd, perhaps, especially in front of other people. He gets to his partner through a slow but steady stream of low level assaults..."

The emotional damage caused by narcissistic abuse is cumulative, which is one of the reasons why the abuse is so hard to pinpoint. We often don't recognize or become alarmed at what appears small and harmless in a particular moment. Most of us would be quick to state: "No one is perfect." We do not suspect we're being used, deceived, or conned. We assume the best intentions from the people who claim to love us. The lack of public awareness and education blinds us from seeing the pieces of our self-esteem and identity slowly being chipped away.

It is challenging enough to try to describe what narcissistic abuse is, but even more challenging to try to spark the concern of people who haven't experienced it. Some may feel they are too smart or too strong for it to ever happen to them, or impact their life in any way.

A commonly held misconception is that only weak-minded, fragile, co-dependent types are vulnerable to being abused. Sadly, this stereotype only heightens the danger of the current lack of public awareness, and provides a false sense of protection.

The damage caused by narcissistic abuse is not limited to the individual victim. It permeates into society and impacts us all. Numerous studies advise us about the correlation between psychological and emotional stress, and its relationship to increased risk of illness and disease. The chronic stress of narcissistic abuse gradually wears our bodies down over time. This prolonged stress can take its toll and wreak havoc on our physiology, and overall well-being. Some common illnesses attributed with the chronic stress of narcissistic abuse include heart attack, adrenal fatigue, weight gain or loss, hair loss, insomnia, anxiety, depression, suicidal thoughts, PTSD, autoimmune disorders, digestive problems, asthma, migraines, epilepsy, cancer, arthritis, slower wound healing, Type II Diabetes, high cholesterol, IBS, and increased dependency on alcohol, drugs, food, or other substances.

Consequently, many victims wind up missing work due to illness, or are laid off from their jobs because of excessive absences or poor work performance. As a result, some are forced to rely on taxpayer funded government and state programs, such as disability, low-income housing, welfare, food stamps, etc. Children who are victims of narcissistic abuse often perform poorly academically, act out, and develop behavioral and/or substance abuse issues. Instead of receiving proper care and treatment for abuse, these children are identified as "behavioral problems," and placed in federally funded discipline and safety programs. The financial costs narcissistic abuse places on society would unarguably be more wisely and effectively spent if we were to use those funds for public awareness and education.

## Symptoms

Narcissism has a long laundry list of symptoms, albeit not all are present at any given moment. Ladies, see if any of these are things you have seen in your partner.

The most prominent symptom is that of having a grandiose sense of self importance and requiring excessive admiration. He can become so preoccupied with fantasies of unlimited success, power, brilliance, beauty, or ideal love, that he considers himself 'special' or unique - so much so that he tends to exaggerate his achievements and talents, and expects to be recognized a superior without commensurate achievements. He feels he can only be understood by, or should only associate with other special or high status people or institutions. This perceived level of intimacy with these higher ups is just that - perceived. Quite sad, don't you think?

The narcissist also has a very strong sense of entitlement. He has unreasonable expectations of especially favorable treatment or automatic compliance and obedience. He insists others see him as he wishes to be seen, even by force. He seeks to establish abusive power and control by callously and arrogantly belittling others in order to validate his own superiority and protect himself, which is either done purposefully or unknowingly. When he realizes his comments have hurt someone, he reacts with contempt and views this as a sign of weakness. He tends to monopolize conversations about himself and becomes impatient or disdainful with others when they talk about themselves. He is so self absorbed that he feels others are envious of him, but in reality is often envious of others.

You see, the common misconception is that the narcissist loves himself. He actually dislikes himself immensely and won't admit it, but will cover it up with self-flattery and arrogance. This self-loathing is projected outward in his disdain for and criticism of others. He is too afraid to look at himself because he believes the truth would be devastating. Emotionally he may be dead inside and is hungering to be validated by others. Ironically he is unable to appreciate the love he does get and he alienates those who give it.

He hides his inadequacies at all cost, masking his feelings from others with feigned humility, by isolating himself from others, or he may react with outbursts of rage, defiance, or revenge. Because his ego, self-esteem and self-concept are fragile and hypersensitive to perceived criticism or defeat, he is prone to feelings of shame, humiliation, and worthlessness over minor or even imagined incidents. His typical reaction is anger which, although can be disproportionate to the situation, is manifested by deliberate and calculated actions and responses. He has occasional flare-ups of insecurity, but his self-image remains stable. In reality, the narcissist is prone to bouts of depression, bipolar disorder, anorexia, substance abuse (especially cocaine), and other addictive behaviors.

Professionally speaking, the narcissist usually has a high level of functionality and, not surprising, may not view himself as having an impairment in his life. This overconfidence makes him ambitious, but this ambition does not necessarily lead to success and professional high achievement. He may be unwilling to compete or refuse to take risks in order to avoid appearing like a failure. Instead of compelling him to improve himself, his inability to tolerate setbacks, disagreements, criticism, and lack of empathy makes it difficult to work cooperatively with others or maintain long-term professional (or any other type of) relationships.

**A Relationship with a Narcissist**

What is a day in the life with a narcissist like? Of course, situations vary from person to person, but most have some of these commonalities. Do any resonate with you?

The initial romance goes so very well! He showers you with attention and seems to be so "in tune" with your needs. He has his agenda, though. He expects appreciation of his specialness. He also expects specific responses through demands and criticism in order to manage his internal environment and protect against his high sensitivity, humiliation and shame. In all reality, relationships really revolve around him, and he experiences his partner as an extension of himself and not as her own person.

Nothing you or others do is right or appreciated because the narcissist is a perfectionist. Even though she can do no right in his eyes, she is expected to know and meet his endless needs, without his having to ask, and she is dismissed when she does not meet his mark. Trying to please him is thankless (like trying to fill a bottomless pit) and subsequently leaves you feeling tense and drained from unpredictable tantrums, attacks, false accusations, criticism, and unjustified indignation about small or imaginary slights. You daily risk blame and punishment, love being withheld, or a rupture in the relationship. He manipulates to get his way and punishes or tries to make his partner feel guilty for turning him down. Inevitably she has to fit into the narcissist's cold world and get used to living with emotional abandonment. Soon she begins to doubt herself and lose confidence and self-worth (a result of gaslighting, which will be discussed in the next chapter). Communicating her disappointment is of no use because it often gets twisted and she is met with defensive blame or further put-downs. Sometimes those eggshells we walk on feel like shards of glass!

So why would any woman (or anyone, for that matter) stay with a narcissist? Periodically the charm, excitement, and loving gestures that first enchanted them return, especially when the narcissist feels threatened that a breakup is imminent. When they sense you trying to regain your control from them, they respond with turning on the charm so that you'll "fall in love" with them all over again. Once they see they have your heart again, they return to their real persona.

For the narcissist, getting emotionally close means giving up power and control. The thought of being dependent is abhorrent. It not only limits his options and makes him feel weak, but also exposes him to rejection and feelings of shame, which he keeps from consciousness at all costs. His anxious partner pursues him, unconsciously replaying emotional abandonment from his past. The result is that both feel unlovable.

So how does one successfully handle a narcissist? Some of what I'm about to share with you may seem harsh to some. Please do not misinterpret my intentions, but my sincerest hope and prayer is that you will read these suggestions with an open mind and heart, accept and internalize them. I want you to see your situation for what it is, not what your vision of it could be. These will help you keep your sanity!

Please understand and accept that YOUR NEEDS WILL NOT BE FULFILLED OR EVEN RECOGNIZED. The narcissist looks for obedient admirers who will tell him how great he is to prop up his insatiable ego. YOUR DESIRES AND FEELINGS DO NOT COUNT.

Look at how the narcissist treats others. If he lies, manipulates, hurts and disrespects others, he will eventually do the same to you. DO NOT THINK YOU ARE DIFFERENT AND WILL BE SPARED OF HIS DEGRADING BEHAVIOR.

IT IS CRUCIAL TO SEE THE NARCISSIST FOR WHO HE IS AND NOT WHO YOU WANT HIM TO BE. Jeremiah

17:9 tells us we are to guard our hearts because it is deceitful above all things and desperate. The heart sees what it wants to see. So stop making excuses for his bad behavior or minimizing the hurt it is causing you! Denial won't make it go away. The reality is that narcissists are very resistant to change, so THE TRUE QUESTION TO ASK YOURSELF IS WHETHER YOU CAN LIVE LIKE THIS INDEFINITELY.

DO NOT TAKE THINGS PERSONALLY. Don't buy into the narcissist's version of who you are and allow it to undermine your self-esteem. Don't argue or engage with a narcissist because he cannot hear you and only wants to wear you down. This is a control tactic. Tell him you disagree and move on. It will be much easier to reject any unfair criticisms leveled against you when you know your own strengths and weaknesses. If you're not sure what these are, ask someone you trust who knows you well or, better yet, ask God. Be okay with knowing the truth about yourself and let go of the need for approval by detaching from the narcissist's opinion. Remember that he projects his negative view of himself onto others, so this opinion is very skewed and completely incorrect.

Now that we've swallowed that hard pill (gulp!), let's look at some positive strategies you can put into place today!

FOCUS ON YOUR OWN DREAMS. Instead of losing yourself in the narcissist's delusions, focus on the things you want for yourself. What do you want to change in your life? What gifts would you like to develop? What purpose do you want God to fulfill through you? What fantasies do you need to give up in order to create a more fulfilling reality?

SET HEALTHY BOUNDARIES. The narcissist is not capable of having a healthy relationship with anyone else based on mutual respect and caring. He does not see, hear, or recognize anyone who exists outside of his own needs. He therefore regularly violates the boundaries of others with absolute sense of entitlement, i.e. going through, "borrowing," giving away or even selling your possessions without asking; eavesdropping; stealing your ideas; telling you what you think and feel.

There are several things to keep in mind when setting boundaries with narcissists. Should you want to maintain a relationship with the narcissist, you may want to try a gentle approach. You should also not set a boundary unless you are willing to keep it. Be prepared for other changes in the relationship because he will feel threatened by your wanting to take your control back. And very important, DON'T BACK DOWN NO MATTER HOW MUCH THEY REBEL!!

LOOK FOR SUPPORT AND PURPOSE ELSEWHERE. After being in a controlling environment, learning what healthy relationships look and feel like can do wonders for healing. It can be tempting to stay in a dysfunctional relationship because it has become "comfortable," although it makes you feel bad. IN A HEALTHY, RECIPROCAL RELATIONSHIP, YOU WILL FEEL RESPECTED, LISTENED TO, AND FREE TO BE YOURSELF. This begins with making new friends outside the narcissist's circle. Some narcissists isolate the people in their lives in order to better control them. Invest time into rebuilding lapsed friendships or cultivating new ones. Looking for meaning and purpose in work, volunteering and hobbies, along with pursuing meaningful activities that make use of your talents and allows you to contribute are very conducive to rediscovering yourself.

Narcissism in itself is a very ugly creature, isn't it? But it has an even uglier first cousin: gaslighting.

## CHAPTER 7:

# Gaslighting – No, You're Not Going Crazy!

So what exactly is gaslighting? It is the psychological manipulation based on the need for power, control, or concealment to sow seeds of doubt so that you question your memory, perception, and sanity. It is the emotional abuse that slowly eats away at your ability to make judgments, deflecting the blame for the perpetrator's abusive deeds, and point the finger at you. YOU ULTIMATELY REALIZE YOU ARE A SHELL OF YOUR FORMER SELF. Incidentally, this is a common technique used by abusers, dictators, narcissists, and cult leaders.

Some very common signs of gaslighting is that you notice something is "off" about your partner, you feel threatened, on edge and scared around this person, as though something is terribly wrong, but you can't quite explain or pinpoint what or why. This can leave you feeling like you are constantly overreacting, confused, disoriented, or too sensitive.

You frequently second guess your ability to remember the details of past events, leaving you psychologically powerless. As a result, you find it hard to trust your own judgment and, if given a choice, you choose to believe the judgment of the abuser. You never quite feel "good enough" and try to live up to the expectations and demands of the abuser, even if they are unreasonable or harm you in some way, therefore you find yourself apologizing all the time for what you do or who you are. You can even feel like there's something fundamentally wrong with you, like feeling you're neurotic or you're "losing it."

You feel as though you are a much weaker version of yourself, and you were stronger and more confident in the past. You therefore become afraid of speaking up or expressing your emotions, so you stay silent instead. This can leave you feeling guilty for not feeling happy like you used to. It can also lead to feeling isolated, hopeless, misunderstood and depressed.

**Tactics Used by Gaslighters**

How can anyone feel so completely awful about themselves that they actually question their own sanity? Gaslighters use a number of interesting strategies that can affect their victims to that exact extreme.

Let's examine a few. A warning, you may find these very appalling, but I'm just trying to present facts. Have you ever felt that you get funny stares from the friends of the narcissist in your life, like as if they're trying to figure out if there's any truth to what they had been told by the narcissist? I can relate! It's because the narcissist tries to discredit you by making others think you're crazy, irrational, or unstable. You get the funny stares because most of the time, these people don't see any evidence of what they've been told. Score: You=1, Narcissist=0.

He'll use a mask of confidence, assertiveness, and/or fake compassion to make you believe that you "have it all wrong." When he confidently and subtly twists and reframes in his favor what was said or done, he can cause you to second-guess yourself, especially when paired with fake compassion, making you feel as though you're unstable or irrational, and begin believing his version of past events.

To add insult to injury, he will trivialize how you feel and what you think; in doing so, he gains more power over you. He can make statements like, "why are you being so sensitive?" "You don't need to get angry over a little thing like that!" "I was just joking around. Why are you taking things so seriously?"

He will also use denial and avoidance to refuse to acknowledge your thoughts and feelings. This can cause you to doubt yourself more. He can say things like, "I don't remember that. You must have dreamt it." "You're lying. I never said that." "I don't know what you're talking about. You're changing the subject."

Speaking of changing the subject, this is something the gaslighter loves to do to avoid the negative spotlight on himself. He will divert the topic by asking another question, or by making a statement usually directed at your thoughts. Sample statements can include, "You're imagining things. That never happened." "No, you're wrong. You didn't remember correctly." "Is that another crazy idea you got from (family member/friend)?"

These are some very cruel tactics that are deliberate in producing the effect the gaslighter is after - you questioning your own rationale and even sanity. These wounds can run very long and deep, but they can be healed.

Knowledge and awareness are the first steps to healing and rebuilding. Even though we have all experienced one form of gaslighting or another in life, problems arise when it is a frequent shadow that trails our relationships and partnerships. Therefore clarifying to yourself how and when you're being gaslighted is very important. Think about what ways he makes you feel unhinged and like you're losing it. Listen to your instinct or intuition. Write down whatever you can think of. Do you have a heavy feeling in the pit of your stomach? Do you feel weighed down, oppressed, or depressed?

These are signs you have unconsciously picked up on deception and foul play. You must be able to confirm you're being gaslighted before you can move on with your life. We can't unconsciously be fooled and we often have a lingering feeling that something isn't quite right. Listen to this feeling and seek help - professionally or socially (i.e. a trusted group of friends, support network, etc.).

Pay attention to these signs of being gaslighted: feeling confused, belittled, crazy, manipulated. Take a deep breath, clear your mind, and center yourself. Set aside regular time for grounding each day. This will help you stay objective in difficult circumstances. Prayer changes things, if only for your own peace and clarity.

An important decision you will need to make is whether you feel it's worth continuing your relationship. It this is going on at work, think about whether it's worth staying at your job or not. If you want to stay in the relationship, think about ways to minimize interaction with the gaslighter until you feel grounded and confident.

Another important action you will need to take is to shift your perspective from being a victim to being a warrior, winner, or whatever word feels the most empowering to you. You don't have to remain a victim for the rest of your life, and by reclaiming your personal power, YOU WILL ALSO BE ABLE TO HELP OTHERS IN SIMILAR SITUATIONS.

## CHAPTER 8:

# Emotional Intelligence – Who Has It?

So what exactly is emotional intelligence (EI), and what does it have to do with narcissism? EI is defined as the capacity of individuals to recognize their own emotions and those of others, to discern between different feelings and label them appropriately, to use emotional information to guide thinking and behavior, and to manage and/or adjust emotions to adapt to environments or achieve one's goals.

Emotional intelligence is the foundation for critical skills and is made up of the following qualities: decision-making, time management, stress tolerance, anger management, trust, empathy, assertiveness, presentation skills, teamwork, change tolerance, communication, social skills, accountability, customer service, flexibility, and loyalty. Some of these qualities will be further dissected.

People with EI are able to relate problems to internal emotional experience. This personalization of problems makes them more meaningful in that they have become more personally relevant (i.e. taking ownership and responsibility for actions).

More than showing empathy, people with EI have the capacity to perceive emotions, to assimilate emotion-related feelings, and to understand and manage information that is the consequence of those emotions. They can also regulate emotion by monitoring, evaluating, and, if required, altering emotion.

Problem-solving skills in emotional intelligence include enhanced memory organization, more creative thinking, confidence, and ability to sort issues more effectively. People with EI demonstrate eagerness and perseverance in the face of obstacles.

How do narcissists measure up to these standards? They overestimate their EI, but in reality have very low EI because of being impulsive, overly critical, and have unrealistic expectations.

## Can Emotional Intelligence be Learned and Developed?

The good news is yes, it can! This is done by unlearning old patterns of thoughts, feelings and actions. This process will require motivation, dedication, time, effort, and practice by the narcissist. A word of caution - the sincerity of the narcissist's commitment must be questioned.

To begin, there are a number of essential social and emotional skills that would need to be addressed. These include: communicating effectively; working cooperatively with others; exhibiting emotional self-control and appropriate expression; displaying empathy and perspective taking; exhibiting optimism, humor, and self-awareness; having the ability to plan and set goals; solving problems and resolving conflicts thoughtfully and nonviolently; and bringing a selective, learning-to-learn approach to all domains of life.

So how does one go about tackling these skills? For one, EI development must focus on life skills and social competencies; health promotion and problem behavior prevention skills; coping skills, conflict resolution, and social support for transitions and crises; and positive, contributory service. Here's the play-by-play.

In order to develop these skills, a skill must first be identified. A rational use for it must then be created and discussed. This would include modeling and teaching components of the skill and their integration. Activities for practice and opportunity for feedback must be provided, and prompts and cues that can assist in adapting those skills to other settings must also be established. These methods can be incorporated by utilizing role-playing, journals, and checklists.

It has been well established that narcissists do not respond well to stressful situations. The following practice skills can be implemented to help them respond appropriately. First he must recognize the stressful feeling and shift his attention away from the disturbing emotion. He can then practice being calm and be directed to re-experience a previous positive emotion. The goal would be to have him ask himself what could be a more effective response to the stressful situation and subsequently follow through.

An effective emotional intelligence training strategy should include the following components (please keep in mind that the narcissist must show SINCERE DEDICATION to his recovery - otherwise it will just be further manipulation on his part):

- Setting expectations and goals to avoid frustration. Having the narcissist restate these expectations in his own words is a good way of establishing a shared understanding. Assistance may be needed in setting expectations so that the narcissist does not feel overwhelmed. Specific goals should be discussed and negotiated with a willingness to compromise if necessary.

- Putting an accessible support structure in place helps the narcissist feel comfortable approaching you and avoids mistrust and undermined loyalty. Being accessible involves being active. This helps dissipate anger and regain self-control, thus acting appropriately. Private conversations involving superior listening skills, empathy and sincerely felt suggestions on how to improve the situation can go a long way.

# PART III

## CHAPTER 9:

# Your Healing

Whenever we board an airplane, part of the safety demonstration involves explaining if there is decreased air pressure in the cabin, oxygen masks will deploy from above each passenger's seat. The flight attendant stresses that, if traveling with a child, the passenger must put on her mask FIRST before assisting the accompanying child. This is the same when dealing with narcissism.

If the narcissist shows genuine promise of turning over a new leaf, the only way you'd be able to support him on this long journey of transformation is to be transformed yourself first. This too will take some time, as much damage has been done and must be undone.

We already know the thoughts that come to mind when we're being abused by the narcissist. We start believing we are worthless, ugly, and have nothing positive to contribute. These thoughts affect our feelings and we become withdrawn and depressed. This, in turn, affects our actions - isolating yourself from friends and family out of fear or shame, then buffering your feelings by overindulging in food, alcohol, or other self-abusing behaviors. Hence, the outcome is not pretty...and we start the cycle all over again the next time he attacks us. But what if we were to throw a wrench in this chain?

Unfortunately, we cannot change our situation because we cannot control another person's behavior (then we'd be the narcissist!). But we can achieve a different outcome if we alter our thoughts, feelings and actions.

We've already established that the narcissist projects his negative self-perception on us, which produce our own negative thoughts of ourselves. Would it make a difference if we knew what others think of us, someone we truly love and loves us? What if that someone were God? What if He tells us not to be anxious because He cares for us, calls us His children, and has good thoughts towards us to give us a future and a hope (Philippians 4:6-9; 1 Peter 5:6-7; 1 John 3:1; Jeremiah 29:11-14)? Would He bother telling us any of these things if He didn't think highly of each of us? If we were to see ourselves through His eyes, would this change the way we think of ourselves and subsequently change our feelings and then our actions? Wouldn't this, therefore produce a very different outcome?

Why would God go through all this trouble? Obviously He loves each of us very much - so much so that He sent His Son to die for us. But He also created each of us with a purpose - for His Kingdom! We each have a place in His Kingdom, but what soldier can take his place in battle formation if he feels depressed and unsure of himself? The outcome would be disastrous. Our Father therefore equips us with the tools necessary to become strong for Him and His Kingdom: His Word, His Son's example and blood, and His Spirit.

Aren't you at least a little bit curious as to what His purpose is for you specifically? Whatever it is, it is a marvelous one!

Are you up for the challenge? Then let's start the healing process - His way. It's time to begin your beautiful transformation and become who you were purposed to be!

This would be where I would insert my 5-step program so you can begin this transformational journey on your own. But I don't want you to take this journey on your own. Part of the healing process is having a positive support system. Allow me to be your number one cheerleader and share this journey with you. You will be more and more enlightened and empowered with each step and have an interchange of triumphs and trepidations with me. You will begin to feel your strength and confidence building, at the same time holding your hand throughout.

Sign up for a free 30 minute consultation on my website vipwomenslifecoaching.com and let's get this transformation underway!

# CHAPTER 10:

# Final Words...

You may be thinking to yourself, "God's kingdom? That's so far off." My sisters, it may be much closer than you think!

Malachi 4 talks about the day of judgment, which we know to be Christ's second coming. For those who fear His name, this will be the day of deliverance. Verses 5 and 6 indicate that Elijah must come before this "great and terrible day of the Lord", to reconcile parents and children, and gather all to Christ (Malachi 4:5-6, World Messianic Bible). This had an initial fulfillment when John the Baptist paved the way for the Messiah's arrival. But that wasn't His great and terrible day of judgment; this is yet to come.

Can you imagine what it must have been like to be a follower of John and be led to Christ? I want to be a follower of the one whom God sends as Elijah. This one will reveal all truth and initiate the greatest ingathering of God's children ever done. I want to be there! I want to be a part of this! This Elijah will set all matters straight, including all injustices done to women. It would not surprise me, therefore, if Elijah turns out to be a woman!!

My sisters, when this day comes, when Elijah arrives, will you be ready? Will you be free of whatever binds and controls you? Allow God to break all your chains so you will be ready and standing firm on that wonderful day!!

May our God and His Christ be glorified forever!!

# References

American Psychiatric Association. (2013). Personality Disorders. In Diagnostic and Statistical Manual of Mental Disorders (Fifth Edition ed.). Washington, DC: American Psychiatric Publishing Inc.

Bancroft, Lundy (2003). Why Does He Do That?: Inside the Minds of Angry and Controlling Men New York: Berkey, Print.

Brown, S.L., MA. (2010, August 08). 60 Million Persons in the U.S. Negatively Affected by Someone Else's Pathology. https://www.psychologytoday.com/blog/pathological-relationships/20100860-million-people-in-the-us-negatively-affected-by-someone-elses-pathology.

Burgess, L. (2018, January 4). "What Are Cluster B Personality Disorders?." Medical News Today.

Johnson, J.G., Cohen, P., Smailes, E.M., Skodol, A.E., Brown, J., Oldham, J.M. (2001, January. Vol 42, Issue 1, Pages 16-23.) Childhood Verbal Abuse and Risk for Personality Disorders

During Adolescence and Early Adulthood. Comprehensive Psychiatry.

Personality Disorders. (2017). In Diagnostic and Statistical Manual of Mental Disorders (pp.659-672). Washington DC: American Psychiatric Publishing.

Perugula, M.L., Narang, P.D., and Lippmann, S.B. (2017). The Biological Basis to Personality Disorders. The Primary Care Companion for CNS Disorders.

Ronningstam, E., & Weinberg, I. (2013, Spring). Narcissistic Personality Disorder: Progress in Recognition and Treatment. The Journal of Lifelong Learning in Psychiatry, XII(2), 167-177.

Schulte, L., Dziobek, I., Cater, A., Heekeren, H.R., Bajboul, M., Renneberg, B., Heuser, I., and Roepke, S. (2013, October. Volume 47, Issue 10). Journal of Psychiatric Research.

South, S.C., and Reichborn-Kjennerud, T. (2017, March 06) Genetics of Personality Disorders. Wiley Online Library.

Printed in the USA
CPSIA information can be obtained
at www.ICGtesting.com
LVHW092009300124
770322LV00004B/148